INDIAN FABLES

INDIAN FABLES

EDITED BY

P. V. RAMASWAMI RAJU

Plates by F. CARRUTHERS GOULD

GYAN

Published by

Gyan Publishing House
5, Ansari Road
Daryaganj, New Delhi-110002
Phone: 011-47034999, 9811692060
E-mail: books@gyanbooks.com

Distribution Network
gyanbooks.com
India, USA, Canada, UK, Australia, France

ISBN: 978-81-212-8682-4 (PB)
First Published, 1887

2nd Impression 2023

Printed at: Gyan Press, Delhi.

INDIAN FABLES
Editor: P. V. Ramaswami Raju

INDIAN FABLES

INDIAN FABLES

COLLECTED AND EDITED BY

P. V. RAMASWAMI RAJU,

B.A., M.R.A.S., F.R.H.S.,

Of the Inner Temple, Barrister-at-Law; Tamil and Telugu Lecturer at University College, London; and late Telugu Lecturer at Oxford.

With 18 Plates by F. CARRUTHERS GOULD.

London:

SWAN SONNENSCHEIN & CO., LIM.

PATERNOSTER SQUARE

1901

First Edition, June, 1887; *Second Edition*, June, 1901.

PREFACE.

WHATEVER diversity of opinion there may be concerning matters oriental among the races inhabiting the West, there has been one point on which it may be said that but one view has been entertained by them all—that the East is the original abode of much of the Fable and Romance that have formed the heirloom of this world.

Hence, some have been inclined to think that when Æsop gave his immortal collection of Fables to the world, he might have derived the bulk of his material from an Eastern source. In more recent times, not a few have surmised that the highly admired collection of tales known as the Arabian Nights' Entertainments, though ostensibly derived from the people of Arabia, might have been obtained by that very people, like many of their arts and sciences, from a more remote centre of Eastern learning.

This great capacity of the Far East to furnish materials for Fables and Romances in endless variety is as much a characteristic of it now as in days of antiquity. To one that has the time and inclination to collect such materials, there is no better field than India. The proverbs and pithy sayings—not to speak of other crude germs, capable of development into fables with wholesome morals, which abound among the people of the country—are, in the metaphorical language of many of its writers, "as many as the pearls of the deep." But these pearls lie underneath the surface, and sometimes "full many a fathom deep."

Hence it is that many a person that has traversed the country from the Himalaya to Cape Comorin has failed to see them. Nay, many that have spent years in India have, like many seafaring men that have spent their lives on the ocean wave, failed to see them at all.

Like the few that specially dive for them, some have from time to time endeavoured to collect the materials described above, and presented them in the shape of works which have interested the public.

Their labours, instead of exhausting the materials, have only proved their extent, even as all the divers for the wealth of the seas heretofore have, instead of exhausting it, only proved the extent to which mankind may profit by continuing their labours in that direction.

The efforts that I have made to collect the materials for these Fables, and present them in this form, have to be regarded, more or less, in this light. The work that is now submitted to the public is the outcome of continued research during a number of years. How far they may be interesting or instructive I leave it to the judgment of the general reader and the critic to decide.

The collection contains more than a hundred fables. Of these a few have long had a standing in the literature of India, though in a slightly different garb. The rest may be said to have been derived from original sources.

During the past two years these Fables, with illustrations, have been before the public in the columns of *The Leisure Hour*.

The volume has been dedicated to Sir William Andrew, whose great interest in such pursuits, and especially in matters concerning India, is well known to all. His brief yet valuable letter accepting the dedication, containing, in addition to his impression of the character of the work, an expression of that genuine regard and sympathy which he has invariably entertained towards the people of India, is reproduced here in the hope that the perusal of it may prove a source of gratification to the British public and to my countrymen in India.

LETTER FROM SIR WILLIAM ANDREW, C.T.E.

"29, BRYANSTON SQUARE, W.

"MY DEAR SIR,—

"I accept with much pleasure the dedication of your interesting volume of Fables from the Far East. Such a dedication from a Hindu gentleman of your ability is peculiarly gratifying to me, from having paid so much attention to India and the interesting people who inhabit that vast empire.

"I return herewith the manuscript, the perusal of which has afforded me much gratification.

"Believe me, yours very truly,

"W. P. ANDREW.

"P. V. RAMASWAMI RAJU, Esq."

CONTENTS.

INDIAN FABLES.

THE GLOW-WORM AND THE DAW.

A JACKDAW once ran up to a glow-worm and was about to seize him. "Wait a moment, good friend," said the worm; "and you shall hear something to your advantage."

"Ah! what is it?" said the daw.

"I am but one of the many glow-worms that live in this forest. If you wish to have them all, follow me," said the glow-worm.

"Certainly!" said the daw.

Then the glow-worm led him to a place in the wood where a fire had been kindled by some woodmen, and pointing to the sparks flying about, said, "There you find the glow-worms warming themselves

B

round a fire. When you have done with them, I shall show you some more, at a distance from this place."

The daw darted at the sparks, and tried to swallow some of them; but his mouth being burnt by the attempt, he ran away exclaiming, "Ah, the glow-worm is a dangerous little creature!"

Said the glow-worm with pride, "*Wickedness yields to wisdom!*"

THE KING AND HIS VASSAL.

AN Eastern king was very angry with a certain chieftain who had not seen him at court, though often desired to do so. One day he was walking through the streets of his capital in disguise with his chief minister, according to the custom of kings in the East, to see how the people fared. Soon after passing a butcher's shop, the king said to his minister, "Instantly the chieftain arrives in the city, send him up to me."

When the minister returned to his palace, he found the chieftain on his way to the court. "Pray, don't see his Majesty till I ask you to do so; and don't ask me for the reason now," said the minister to the chieftain, who therefore postponed his visit.

The king came to know of this, and asked the minister why he had done so.

"Sire," said the minister, "your order to send up the chieftain was given after passing a butcher's shop, and you meant to flay him like a sheep; so I asked him to see you some time after, when you should be in a better mood to see him."

The king confessed his intention, and said, "*A wise minister is a tyrant's curb.*"

THE FOX AND THE VILLAGERS.

A FOX that had long been the dread of the village poultry yard was one day found lying breathless in a field. The report went abroad that, after all, he had been caught and killed by some one. In a moment, everybody in the village came out to see the dead fox. The village cock, with all his hens and chicks, was also there, to enjoy the sight.

The fox then got up, and, shaking off his drowsiness, said, "I ate a number of hens and chicks last night; hence I must have slumbered longer than usual."

The cock counted his hens and chicks, and found a number wanting. "Alas!" said he, "how is it I did not know of it?"

"My dear sir," said the fox, as he retreated to the wood, "it was last night I had a good meal on your hens and chicks, yet you did not know of it. A moment ago they found me lying in the field, and you knew of it at once. *Ill news travels fast!*"

THE LION, THE STAG, AND THE FOX.

A fox saw a stag, and exclaimed, "What rich meat there is in him!"

A lion, that had got nothing to eat for some time, was prowling at a distance.

The fox said to himself, "If I should point out the stag to the lion, he will make his breakfast off him, and leave me the remainder." So he went up to the lion and, bowing respectfully, said, "If your majesty will step in that way, your majesty's humble servant will be able to point out something highly desirable."

"Very good!" said the lion, and followed the fox.

But the stag, who had got a hint of the conspiracy, ran up to a place of safety, and was watching their movements unseen.

The lion, not finding the stag, said to the fox, "Knave, you have deceived me! I am frantically hungry: you are as good a morsel as the stag, though a trifle less in size," and, springing on him, ate him up in no time.

Said the stag, "*The wicked are often caught in their own toils.*"

TINSEL AND LIGHTNING.

A PIECE of tinsel on a rock once said to a pebble, "You see how bright I am! I am by birth related to the lightning."

"Indeed!" said the pebble; "then accept my humble respects."

Some time after, a flash of lightning struck the rock, and the tinsel lost all its brilliancy by the scorching effects of the flash.

"Where is your brilliancy now?" said the pebble.

"Oh, it is gone to the skies," said the tinsel, "for I have lent it to the lightning that came down a moment ago to borrow it of me."

"Dear me!" said the pebble; "*how many fibs doth good bragging need!*"

THE MONKEY AND THE LOOKING-GLASS.

A MONKEY in a wood somehow got a looking-glass, and went about showing it to the animals around him. The bear looked into it and said he was very sorry he had such an ugly face. The wolf said he would fain have the face of a stag, with its beautiful horns. So every beast felt sad that it had not the face of some other in the wood.

The monkey then took it to an owl that had witnessed the whole scene. "No," said the owl, "I would not look into it, for I am sure, in this case as in many others, knowledge is but a source of pain."

"You are quite right," said the beasts, and broke the glass to pieces, exclaiming, "*Ignorance is bliss!*"

THE FAWN AND THE LITTLE TIGER.

A FAWN met a little tiger, and said, "What fine stripes you have!"

The little tiger said, "What fine spots you have!"

Then the fawn said, "It would be such a nice thing if you and I were to live together as friends. We might then roam through the woods as we like, and be so happy!"

"I think so too," said the tiger.

The two joined hands, and went out for a long walk. It was breakfast time. The fawn saw some fine grass in the lawn, and said to himself, "One should first see his friend fed and then feed." So he turned to the tiger and said, "Will you have some of this fine grass for your breakfast?"

The tiger put his nose to the grass; but could not bring himself to feed upon it, because it was against his nature; so he replied, "I am so sorry, I cannot eat it!"

Then the fawn said, "Allow me to go home for one moment and ask mamma for something that would suit you for breakfast."

So the fawn went home and told the hind of the happy friendship he had formed, and of all that had happened since.

The hind replied, "Child, how lucky it is that you have come away! You must know the tiger is the most deadly enemy we have in the woods."

At these words the fawn drew near to his dam and trembled.

The hind said, "*It is indeed lucky to get away from the wicked at the first hint!*"

THE LION, THE FOX, AND THE STAR.

A YOUNG lion and a young fox once went out together for an evening stroll. Venus, the evening star, had just risen. The fox said, "Ah, how I wish I could go to the star and play with it!"

The lion said, "Ah, how I wish the star would come here and play with me!"

An owl, who had heard their words from a neighbouring tree, said, "*The character of each is known by his words!*"

THE SEA, THE FOX, AND THE WOLF.

A FOX that lived by the sea-shore once met a wolf that had never seen the sea. The wolf said, "What is the sea?"

"It is a great piece of water by my dwelling," said the fox.

"Is it under your control?" said the wolf.

"Certainly," said the fox.

"Will you show me the sea, then?" said the wolf.

"With pleasure," said the fox. So the fox led the wolf to the sea, and said to the waves, "Now go back,"—they went back! "Now come up,"—and they came up! Then the fox said to the waves, "My friend, the wolf has come to see you, so you will come up and go back till I bid you stop;" and the wolf saw, with wonder, the waves coming up and going back.

He said to the fox, "May I go into the sea?"

"As far as you like. Don't be afraid, for, at a word, the sea would go or come as I bid, and as you have already seen."

The wolf believed the fox, and followed the waves rather far from the shore. A great wave soon upset him, and threw up

THE FOUR OWLS.

[*Face p.* 11.

his carcass on the shore. The fox made a hearty breakfast on it, saying, "*The fool's ear was made for the knave's tongue.*"

THE FOUR OWLS.

FOUR owls went out, each to a part of the world, to see how people liked things, ill and false, and came back to tell of what they had seen.

The owl that went north said, "I saw, by a stream, the fish make mouths at the birds. They further said, 'Look at our fins and their wings, how queer they are!'"

The owl that went south said, "I saw on a hill a fly of fair hues go by the door of a hive; the bees said, 'Look, he has come to beg of us for some food.' The fly said to a friend of his, 'These rogues, I mean the bees, stole the sweets from the blooms when the air was dry, so now I have naught to eat when it is cold.'"

The owl that went east said, "I saw in a wood a pard go out from his den. The wolf went with him a few yards, came back, and said to a friend of his, 'The pard is a knave, yet I cling to him, for he is strong.'"

The owl that went west said, "I saw a bear pass by a lion's den. A fox close by said the bear went to make love to the lion's mate, but was sent back with a box on his ear."

The four owls together said, "*Where the sun shines, there scandal is.*"

THE TIGER, THE WOLF, AND THE FOX.

A WOLF was often cheated of his prey by a fox; so he thought the best way of getting rid of his enemy would be to carry tales against him to the tiger, who was the king of the forest.

So one fine morning he went to the lair of the king, and said, "Good morning, your majesty."

"What news, my good fellow?" said the king.

THE TIGER, THE BEAR, AND THE FOX.

[*Face p.* 12.

"Ah, I have such news," said the wolf, "as would only increase your anger against that reckless villain Reynard; but, as he is my friend, I think it better to keep it from my sovereign."

This only made the tiger more eager to know what the wolf had to say. He therefore commanded him to disclose all that Reynard had done.

Quoth the wolf, "Yesterday there was a meeting of all the animals in the forest, to confer as to the best method of expressing their gratitude for all the blessings they have received from your majesty. I was anxious to know if there was any among them that had ill-feelings towards my sovereign. So I began by pretending to speak ill of your majesty to Reynard. He instantly replied, 'Oh, I quite agree with you! There is no greater tyrant than our present king. The sooner he is got rid of, the better.' I should have laid the matter at once before your majesty; but, as it was late in the night, I could not do so."

The tiger raged with fury; and sending for Reynard then and there, said, "Villain, did you speak ill of us?"

"I did, your majesty," said the fox.

"Why?" said the tiger, in a thundering voice.

"Because," said the fox, in tones equally loud and furious, pointing to the wolf, "that villain there began to slander the character of my benign sovereign, and I was eager, come what would, to find out what the depth of his malice was!"

The tiger was astonished to see the tables thus turned upon the wolf. He was further at a loss to know who the culprit really was. So he sent them away, with the remark, "*'Tis a villain that cheats a villain best!*"

THE FOX AND THE FARMER'S DOG.

A FOX went into a farmyard to see if any poultry could be got; but, finding the people wary and the yard well secured, he

THE FOX IN THE WELL.

[*Face p.* 15.

was returning with a dejected countenance, when the farmer's dog accosted him thus: "Reynard, where have you been?"

"Ah! Mr. Mastiff," said the fox, "I have just been into the farmyard to see if any of my kindred were there."

"Did you find any?" said the mastiff.

"No, I did not; and that is the reason why I am returning," said the fox, and left the place.

"Ah," muttered the mastiff, "*no liar but hath a plea ready-made for every turn!*"

THE FOX IN THE WELL.

A fox fell into a well, and was holding hard to some roots at the side of it, just above the water. A wolf who was passing by saw him, and said, "Hollo, Reynard, after all you have fallen into a well!"

"But not without a purpose, and not without the means of getting out of it," said the fox.

"What do you mean?" said the wolf.

"Why," said the fox, "there is a drought all over the country now, and the water in this well is the only means of appeasing the thirst of the thousands that live in this neighbourhood. They held a meeting, and requested me to keep the water from going down lower; so I am holding it up for the public good."

"What will be your reward?" said the wolf.

"They will give me a pension, and save me the trouble of going about every day in quest of food, not to speak of innumerable other privileges that will be granted me. Further, I am not to stay here all day. I have asked a kinsman of mine, to whom I have communicated the secret of holding up the water, to relieve me from time to time. Of course he will also get a pension, and have other privileges. I expect him here shortly."

"Ah, Reynard, may I relieve you, then? May I hope to get a pension, and other privileges? You know what a sad lot is mine, especially in winter."

"Certainly," said the fox; "but you must get a long rope, that I may come up and let you in."

So the wolf got a rope. Up came the fox, and down went the wolf, when the former observed, with a laugh, "My dear sir, you may remain there till doomsday, or till the owner of the well throws up your carcass," and left the place.

"Alas!" said the wolf, when it was too late, "*greed hath its meed!*"

THE BIRDS AND THE LIME.

A FOWLER in the East once went to a wood, scattered some grain on the ground, spread a net over it with some lime in it, and was watching from a distance to see what luck would attend his efforts.

A great many birds assembled on the trees around the net, and said, "What fine corn that is! We can seldom hope to get anything like it."

An owl that was close by said, "How nice that white thing in the net is!"

"What is it?" said the birds.

"Why, it is our best friend in the world; it is lime. When it holds us in its embrace, we can never hope to get away."

The birds left the place at once. Said the fowler, "*A clever bird knows the lime!*"

THE WEALTHY MAN AND THE STRING.

A WEALTHY man in the East had no knowledge of music; yet he pretended to know a great deal about it. So, whenever a famous singer came to him, he would tie one end of a string to his coat-tail, and give the other end to his wife, who understood music well, and who generally sat behind a screen, according to the custom of ladies in the East. The understanding was that whenever there was anything in the singing that was specially praiseworthy, the wife should pull, that the man might nod his approbation of it.

Once a great singer was displaying his skill, and suddenly the string snapped. The man cried, " Wait a bit, good singer; the string hath snapped!" The whole audience was amazed, and in the end, knowing what he really meant, exclaimed, "*A parrot and a fool can do nothing without prompting!*"

THE SWORD, THE RAZOR, AND THE STROP.

A RAZOR once said to a sword, " How is it that men always speak of you with respect, while they hardly make any mention of me?"

"Because," said the sword, "you skim over the surface, while I go deeper."

"Just so," said the razor, "and thereby do them more harm than ever I can."

"You are quite right," said the strop, who was of course an ally of the razor;

"men always call those great that do them the largest amount of harm. *The greater the evil, the greater the glory!*"

THE WELL-BRED AND THE ILL-BRED.

A MAN once stood up at a market-place in the East and said, "I have been ordered by the king to collect all the well-born and well-bred and bring them before him, since he wishes to reward them."

Everybody that heard him joined him, and he went towards the palace, surrounded by the whole town. Then he suddenly turned round and said, "The king has just sent me word that he means to help only those that have been ill-born and ill-bred to make up for their misfortunes."

The crowd lingered behind for a while, and then one after another joined the man as ill-born and ill-bred to merit the king's gifts.

The man said, "*The world goes as the wind blows!*"

THE DRUM AND THE SOLDIERS.

A DETACHMENT of soldiers was marching through a wood to avoid meeting a larger detachment of the enemy in the neighbourhood. The drummer kept beating his drum, though not loudly.

The sound, however, attracted the attention of the enemy, and they surrounded the party. The captain bade the drummer beat with all his energy to inspire his men with courage. So he did. They fought like lions, and won the day.

The captain said, "*Good and evil often flow from the same source.*"

THE OWLS AND THE CROWS.

THE owls, who can't see during the day, and the crows, who can't see during the night, were foes. So the owls said to the crows, "We don't want the sun as you do; we can do without him; we can see in the dark."

The crows said, "We don't believe you can see in the dark; those who can't see in the day can much less see in the night."

They became friends. Then the owls said to the crows, "You don't see in the night because you are a part of it; else how could you be so black?"

The crows returned the compliment, saying, "You don't see during the day because your eyes are a part of the sun; else how could they be so brilliant and round?"

Then they said together, "*As we love or hate, we think of each estate!*"

THE FISH AND THE EAGLE.

An eagle once pounced upon a huge fish in a lake, and plunged his talons into his back. The fish pulled downwards, and the eagle upwards. But, neither succeeding in disengaging itself from the other, the fish called all the other fish in the lake to its aid, and the eagle summoned all the birds of the air to its side. The birds pulled the eagle up, and broke its wings. The fish pulled their friend down, and hurt him severely, till in the end both sank exhausted into the lake.

The birds and the fish exclaimed, "*When neither yields in strife, neither can keep his life.* In such cases, friends can only aggravate, in their attempts to alleviate"

THE CAMEL AND THE PIG.

A CAMEL said, "Nothing like being tall! look, how tall I am!"

A pig, who heard these words, said, "Nothing like being short; look, how short I am!"

The camel said, "Well, if I fail to prove the truth of what I said, I shall give up my hump."

The pig said, "If I fail to prove the truth of what I have said, I shall give up my snout."

"Agreed!" said the camel.

"Just so!" said the pig.

They came to a garden, enclosed by a low wall without any opening. The camel stood on this side the wall, and reaching the plants within by means of his long neck, made a breakfast on them. Then he turned jeeringly to the pig, who had been standing at the bottom of the wall, without even having a look at the good things in the garden, and said, "Now, would you be tall, or short?"

Next they came to a garden, enclosed by a high wall, with a wicket gate at one end. The pig entered by the gate, and, after having eaten his fill of the vegetables within, came out, laughing at the poor camel, who had had to stay outside, because he was too tall to enter the garden by the gate, and said, "Now, would you be tall, or short?"

Then they thought the matter over, and came to the conclusion, that the camel should keep his hump and the pig his snout, observing, "*Tall is good, where tall would do; of short, again, 'tis also true!*"

THE FROG AND THE SNAKE.

A SNAKE and a frog were friends in a pond. The snake taught the frog to hiss, and the frog taught the snake to croak. The snake would hide in the reeds and croak. The frogs would say, "Why, there is one of us," and come near. The snake would then dart at them, and eat all he could seize. The frog would hide in the reeds and hiss. His kin would say, "Why, there is the snake," and keep off.

After some time, the frogs found out the trick of the snake, and took care not to come near him. Thus the snake got no frogs to eat for a long time; so he seized his friend to gobble him up.

The frog then said, though too late, "By becoming your friend, I lost the company of my kindred, and am now losing my life. *One's neck to fate one has to bend, when one would make so bad a friend!*"

THE DOVE AND THE GRASSHOPPER.

ONE day a grasshopper was sporting gaily in a green meadow. A dove on an adjacent tree saw it, and, being tempted to eat it, came down. The grasshopper saw the object of the dove, but remained where it was, without moving an inch.

The dove, being surprised at this conduct of his victim, said, "Hollo! how is it you are not afraid of me?"

"Because," said the grasshopper, "you will do me no harm."

This surprised the dove more, and he said, "How so?"

"I'll tell you how; you love your mate, do you not? Well, even so, I love mine. Should a hunter catch you in his net now, would you not be sorry? So, if you should seize me, I should be sorry. If he should let you go, without doing you any harm, would you not be glad? Well, even so, I shall be glad if you let me go without doing me any harm."

These words touched the heart of the dove, and he let the grasshopper go without doing him any harm, saying, "As thou feelest, so do I."

When the good err, tell them so: it helps them, and helps you too.

THE SUN AND THE GLOW-WORM.

A TRAVELLER said, "Ah, how bright the sun is!"

A glow-worm, close by, said, "It is always a quality of our race."

"What do you mean, you impudent little thing?" said the traveller.

The glow-worm replied, "Why, I mean that brightness is ever a quality of the class to which I, the sun, the moon, the stars, and other shining bodies belong!"

"Ah," said the traveller, "*vanity reigns over all creation!*"

THE FOX AND THE CRABS.

ONE day a fox seated himself on a stone by a stream and wept aloud. The crabs in the holes around came up to him and said, "Friend, why are you wailing so loud?"

"Alas!" said the fox, "I have been turned by my kindred out of the wood, and do not know what to do."

"Why were you turned out?" said the crabs, in a tone of pity.

"Because," said the fox, sobbing, "they said they should go out to-night hunting crabs by the stream, and I said it would be a pity to kill such pretty little creatures."

"Where will you go hereafter?" said the crabs.

"Where I can get work," said the fox; "for I would not go to my kindred again, come what would."

Then the crabs held a meeting, and came to the conclusion that, as the fox had been thrown out by his kindred on

THE FOX AND THE CRABS.

[*Face p.* 28.

their account, they could do nothing better than engage his services to defend them. So they told the fox of their intention. He readily consented, and spent the whole day in amusing the crabs with all kinds of tricks.

Night came. The moon rose in full splendour. The fox said, "Have you ever been out for a walk in the moonlight?"

"Never, friend," said the crabs; "we are such little creatures that we are afraid of going far from our holes."

"Oh, never mind!" said the fox; "follow me! I can defend you against any foe."

So the crabs followed him with pleasure. On the way the fox told them all sorts of pleasant things, and cheered them on most heartily. Having thus gone some distance, they reached a plain, where the fox came to a stand, and made a low moan in the direction of an adjacent wood. Instantly a number of foxes came out of the wood and joined their kinsman, and all of them at once set about hunting the poor crabs, who fled in all directions for their lives, but were soon caught and devoured.

When the banquet was over, the foxes said to their friend, "How great thy skill and cunning!"

The heartless villain replied, with a wink, "My friends, *there is cunning in cunning*."

THE ASSEMBLY OF ANIMALS.

ONCE there was a great assembly of the animals in a wood. The lion said, "Look, how great my valour! 'tis this that makes me king of the woods."

The fox said, "Look, how deep my cunning! 'tis this that feeds me so well."

The peacock said, "Look, how bright my feathers! 'tis this that makes me the wonder and admiration of the wood."

The elephant said, "Look, how long and powerful my tusks! there is nothing that can resist them."

A toad, who lived secure in the heart

of a rock, close by, said, "'Tis the lion's valour that leads him to the herds, and gets him killed by the hunters. 'Tis the fox's cunning that brings him to the furrier at last. 'Tis the plumes of the peacock that men covet; hence his ruin. The elephant is hunted for his tusks, and they are his bane. *In the mark of your vanity is your death!*"

THE WORM AND THE SUN.

A WORM that was out in the sun, said, "I wish there was no sun at all. Of what use is he? If he did not shine, I would go far afield, and should be so glad."

A rook that heard this came near and said, "You are quite wrong; the sun is of great use. I should not now have known that you were here but for his light."

With these words he snatched him up in his bill and put him into his craw.

A sage, who saw this, said, "The worm lived but a short while; yet he would have no sun, though all the world wants it. *'Tis hard to deal with minds so low, for love of self is all they know!*"

THE DOG AND THE DOG-DEALER.

A DOG was standing by the cottage of a peasant. A man who dealt in dogs passed by the way. The dog said, "Will you buy me?"

The man said, "Oh, you ugly little thing! I would not give a farthing for you!"

Then the dog went to the palace of the king and stood by the portal. The sentinel caressed it, and said, "You are a charming little creature!"

Just then the dog-dealer came by. The dog said, "Will you buy me?"

"Oh," said the man, "you guard the palace of the king, who must have paid a high price for you. I cannot afford to pay the amount, else I would willingly take you."

"Ah!" said the dog, "*how place and position affect people!*"

THE BANQUET OF THE BEASTS.

THE beasts in a forest once proposed to entertain the lion, their king. They took care not to invite the fox, lest he should somehow mar the proceedings. The fox went to the lion with downcast eyes, and said, "Sire, I am sorry that your subjects have been planning your ruin. They mean to invite you to a feast, and murder you in the midst of the rejoicing. Well knowing that your humble servant is a faithful adherent of his sovereign, they have carefully excluded him from the party."

"How shall we outwit them?" said the lion.

"I request your majesty to accept the invitation," said the fox. "I shall watch unseen somewhere in the neighbourhood, and just as the traitors, under some pretext, advance to attempt your majesty's life, I will make a signal."

"So be it," said the lion.

The entertainment came off. The beasts were in high glee, and spared neither pains nor cost to please the king. There was dancing and music. The peacock danced and the cuckoo sang, and the whole wood resounded with sounds of merriment. The wolf and the hyena, as the chief among the officers of the king, went up to him with a great garland to be placed round his neck, after the fashion in the East on such occasions. The lion bent his neck to receive the present. Just then the fox gave a low howl. Instantly the lion sprang on the wolf and the hyena, and laid them low; the other animals took the hint and fled. The fox joined the lion and pursued them, shouting, "There go the traitors!"

"Alas!" said the beasts, "it is all the doing of that wily fox. We thought we were safe because we had kept him out,

THE BEASTS AND THE FISHES.

[*Face p.* 35.

but it has been quite the other way. *Never lose sight of a knave!*"

THE BEASTS AND THE FISHES.

THE beasts and the fishes once came to an agreement that they should exchange places for some time by way of variety. So the fish ranged over the plains, and the hawks, the kites, the vultures, and other animals soon made dreadful havoc with them.

Most of the beasts that got into the sea, not being able to breathe, soon died by myriads, or were devoured by the sea monsters. So the others with difficulty came to the shore and met the remaining fishes, who had just arrived from the interior of the country.

Said the fishes, "Oh, let us go back to our home, the sea!" and darted into the water.

Said the beasts, "Oh, let us go back to our home, the land!" and jumped ashore.

A sage, who had been witnessing the scene, said, "When will you change places again?"

"Never more! never more!" said both.

Said the sage, "*Each doth best in his own element!*"

THE WISE MAN AND HIS TWO PUPILS.

A WISE man in the East had two pupils, to each of whom he gave, one night, a sum of money, and said, "What I have given you is very little; yet with it you must buy at once something that will fill this dark room."

One of them purchased a great quantity of hay, and cramming it into the room, said, "Sir, I have filled the room."

"Yes," said the wise man, "and with greater gloom."

The other, with scarcely a third of the money, bought a candle, and lighting it said, "Sir, I have filled the hall."

"Yes," said the wise man, "and with

light. *Such are the ways of wisdom, for she seeks good means to good ends.*"

THE LION AND THE CUB.

A YOUNG lion, fond of applause, shunned the company of the lions, and sought that of vulgar and ignoble beasts. He passed all his time with asses. He presided at their meetings; he copied their airs and their manners—in a word, he was an ass in everything except the ears. Elated with vanity, he betook himself to his father's retreat, to display his rare qualities there. He could not but have some that were very ridiculous. He brays, the lion starts.

"Puppy," said he to him, "this disagreeable noise shows what sort of company you have been keeping. Puppies always betray their stupidity."

"Why are you so severe?" asked the young lion. "Our assembly has always admired me."

"How ill-grounded your pride is," replied the father. "You may be sure that *lions despise what asses admire*"

THE PEACOCK, THE GOOSE, AND THE TURKEY.

A PEACOCK was near a barn, along with a goose and a turkey. They regarded the peacock with envious eyes, and made fun of his ridiculous pride. The peacock, conscious of his superior merit, despised their base envy, and shook out the beautiful plumage which dazzled them.

"Look at that conceited bird," said the turkey; "with what pride the creature struts along! Was there ever so conceited a bird? If intrinsic worth were regarded, turkeys have a skin whiter and fairer than this ugly peacock. And see what hideous legs and ugly claws the creature has! And what horrible cries he utters, fit to frighten the very owls."

"It is true," rejoined the peacock,

"these are my defects; you may despise my legs and my voice, but critics like you rail in vain. Know that if my legs supported a goose or a turkey, no one would have noticed such defects in you."

Beauty and merit cause defects to be noticed; but envious people have eyes only to perceive faults.

THE FOOLS AND THE DRUM.

Two fools heard a drum sounding, and said to themselves, "There is some one inside it who makes the noise."

So, watching a moment when the drummer was out, they pierced a hole in each side of it, and pushed their hands in. Each felt the hand of the other within the drum, and exclaimed, "I have caught him!"

Then one said to the other, "Brother, the fellow seems to be a stubborn knave; come what will, we should not give in."

"Not an inch, brother," said the other.

So they kept pulling each other's hand, fancying it was the man in the drum. The drummer came up, and finding them in such an awkward plight, showed them with his fist who the man in the drum really was. But as his fine drum was ruined, he said, with a sigh, "*Alas! fools have fancies with a triple wing!*"

THE FOX AND THE TAME ELEPHANT.

A TAME elephant in the East was once taken to a forest by a party of men to catch wild elephants. A fox said to him, "What a shame that a beast of your size and strength should be led like a cat by men! If I were you, I should at once go back to my kindred."

The elephant thought the words of the fox reasonable, and stole into the forest where the wild elephants lived. They raised their trunks against him, saying, "There comes a traitor to betray us to man."

The elephant replied that he came back to live with them; but they drove him back with curses.

His keeper, seeing that he returned because his kindred had refused to admit him, bound him to a huge tree with chains, and with these words painted on his forehead: "A traitor to his kindred and to his keeper." As often as the wayfarers read these words, the elephant wailed aloud, saying, "*Once a traitor, ever a traitor! A traitor that tries to mend, loses both foe and friend.*"

THE SMITHY.

ONCE words ran high in a smithy.

The furnace said, "If I cease to burn, the smithy must be closed."

The bellows said, "If I cease to blow, no fire, no smithy."

Similarly the hammer and the anvil each claimed to itself the sole credit of keeping up the smithy.

The ploughshare, that had been shaped by their joint efforts, said, "Gentlemen, it is not each that keeps the smithy, but all together. *With but one, good for none. Without the many, no good to any. The world works by combination.*"

THE RAM, THE EWE, AND THE WOLF.

A RAM once said in sport to the ewe and her lamb that, if he chose, he could meet them in the guise of a wolf in broad daylight. A wolf that had been lurking in a neighbouring bush heard this.

The next day, while the sheep were grazing on the plain, the ram strayed to some distance from the sheep and the lamb. The wolf came by another route, and, presenting himself before them, said, "Now you see I am true to my word. I have just taken the guise of a wolf; if you would only go with me to yonder mountain, I can show you more wonders."

They believed his words, and were about to follow him, when the ram came up just in time to point out the mistake. The wolf beat a hasty retreat into the woods.

The ram said to the ewe, "I am indeed sorry for your stupidity. *'Tis a strange sheep that hails in a wolf's guise!*"

THE RAG AND THE RIBBON.

A PIECE of rag, which had somehow got into a king's wardrobe, said to a ribbon on the person of a valet, "What do you think I am?"

"To be sure," said the ribbon, "a piece of rag torn from some old garment."

"I am nothing of the kind," said the rag; "I am a rare ribbon of the cut and colour I am; and the king is proud of having me in his wardrobe."

"What do you think I am?" said the ribbon.

"To be sure," said the other, "a piece

of rag torn from some old garment to suit the fancy of the servant who wears you."

"Alas!" cried the rag, "*Place hides pedigree.*"

THE MAN OF LUCK AND THE MAN OF PLUCK.

A KING in the East said to his minister, "Do you believe in luck?"

"I do," said the minister.

"Can you prove it?" said the king.

"Yes, I can," said the minister.

So one night he tied up to the ceiling of a room a parcel containing peas mixed with diamonds, and let in two men, one of whom believed in luck and the other in human effort alone. The former quietly laid himself down on the ground; the latter after a series of efforts reached the parcel, and feeling in the dark the peas and the stones, ate the former, one by one, and threw down the latter at his companion, saying, "Here are the stones for your idleness." The man below received them in his blanket.

In the morning the king and the minister came to the room and bade each take to himself what he had got. The man of effort found he had nothing beyond the peas he had eaten. The man of luck quietly walked away with the diamonds.

The minister said to the king, "Sire, there is such a thing as luck; but it is as rare as peas mixed with diamonds. So I would say, '*Let none hope to live by luck.*'"

THE THIEF AND THE FOX.

A MAN tied his horse to a tree and went into an inn. A thief hid the horse in a wood, and stood near the tree as if he had not done it.

"Did you see my horse?" said the man.

"Yes," said the thief, "I saw the tree eat up your horse."

"How could the tree eat up my horse?" said the man.

"Why, it did so," said the thief.

The two went to a fox and told him of

the case. The fox said, "I am dull. All last night the sea was on fire; I had to throw a great deal of hay into it to quench the flames; so come to-morrow, and I shall hear your case."

"Oh, you lie," said the thief; "how could the sea burn? how could hay quench the flames?"

"Oh, you lie," said the fox, with a loud laugh; "how could a tree eat up a horse?"

The thief saw his lie had no legs, and gave the man his horse.

THE SNAKE AND THE PARROT.

A SNAKE said to a parrot, "Ah! I really envy you your life; how people fondle you! Why, everybody calls you a pet!"

"Yes," said the parrot, "if you will be as good and kind to people as I am, and try to amuse them as I do, they will treat you also as a pet."

"I will try," said the snake; and, creep-

THE WORKMAN AND THE TREES.

[Face p. 47.

ing to a farmer's door, hissed aloud, as much as to say, "I do not wish to be wicked like other snakes. I wish to be kind and good to you, and amuse you like the parrot."

But the farmer killed the reptile at a stroke, saying, "'Tis quite out of the way, this, for a snake to say!"

Goodness in the wicked is seldom credited.

THE WORKMAN AND THE TREES.

A WOODMAN entered a wood with his axe on his shoulder. The trees were alarmed, and addressed him thus: "Ah, sir, will you not let us live happily some little time longer?"

"Yes," said the woodman, "I am quite willing to do so; but as often as I see this axe, I am tempted to come to the wood, and do my work in it. So I am not so much to blame as this axe."

"We know," said the trees, "that the handle of the axe, which is a piece of the branch of a tree in this very wood, is more to blame than the iron ; for it is that which helps you to destroy its kindred."

"You are quite right," said the woodman ; "*there is no foe so bitter as a renegade.*"

THE ELEPHANT AND THE FLY.

A FLY, who lived in a palace, once said to one of the king's elephants, "Look ! you do such hard work, yet you are confined in a shed, far from the palace ; whereas I do nothing, yet I range over the whole palace and amuse myself where I like, even on the crowned head of the king."

"That is because you are such an insignificant thing," said the elephant.

The fly was abashed, and said, "Alas ! *it signifies nothing where a fly lives !*'

THE MAN AND THE SNAKE.

ONCE a man saw a snake entering his house. His wife, who was at the other end of the house, saw it go out. The man told his wife, " I just saw a snake get into the house : we must find it out."

" I just saw it go out of the house," said the wife ; " so you need not trouble yourself about it."

" Oh, no," said the man ; " you say so because you wish to avoid the trouble of seeking for it."

Then he went about the house in quest of the snake. As he did not find it, he would not eat, nor would he work nor sleep. So she got a dead snake, and, putting it under the cupboard, went up to her husband and said, " Shall we seek for the reptile once more ? "

" Very well," said the man, and went about the house again. He came to the cupboard, and exclaimed, " Ah ! I have found it out, after all ! "

Instantly he had a hearty breakfast, and went to work.

His wife said, as he went out, " He would not have his breakfast till the snake was found out. *Fear works while fancy lurks!*"

THE SPARROW AND THE SEA.

A SPARROW who lived by a pond, in a wood, said to his mate, "In this pond there is neither water nor fish enough; what if we go and live by the sea?"

His mate said, "Yes."

So they went to live by the sea. The sparrow put his bill into the sea, and drank. His mate, finding that he did not take in more water than at the pond, said, "A sparrow drinks more by going to the sea."

"Not so, my love," said the sparrow. "I would drink up the whole sea, but that it is brackish!"

THE SNAKES AND THE EELS.

A KING in the East one day took a walk with his son, a fair young prince, by the

THE OWL AND HIS SCHOOL.

[Face p. 51.

side of a great pond in his park. The prince put his foot in the pond, and a snake coiled round his leg. The king killed the snake, and said to his men, "Kill all the snakes in the pond, and tell me you have done so."

The men, in their haste, could not see which were the snakes and which were the eels. So they killed all, and took them to the king, who said, "What a sad thing!—*the good have died, because they were like the bad in form.*"

THE OWL AND HIS SCHOOL.

An owl named Old Wisdom kept a school. Everybody went to him to take lessons. After some time he wished to know what progress they had made in their studies. So he gave them a number of questions to answer.

The first was, "Why does the moon shine in the sky?"

The nightingale said, "That I might

sing all night in his pleasant light to my bride, the rose."

The lilies said, "That we may open our petals, and enjoy his loving and refreshing beams."

The hare said, "That there may be enough of dew in the morning for me to lap."

The dog said, "That I may find out thieves prowling round my master's house."

The glow-worm said, "That he may throw me into the shade, for he envies my light."

The fox said, "That I may see my way to the poultry-yard."

"Enough!" said Old Wisdom. "There is but one moon that shines in the sky, yet how each brings him to serve his own purpose!" *Self reigns supreme!*

THE COCK AND HIS THREE HENS.

A cock, named Crimson Crest, was once strutting about with his three hens, Meek

Love, Bright Wit, and Fine Feather. The hens, being in very good spirits, said, "Ah, how we love you!"

"Why do you love me at all?" said Crimson Crest.

"Because," said they, "of the noble qualities that adorn your mind."

"Are you sure," said he, "you love me for the qualities that adorn my mind?"

"Yes, we are," said the three with one voice.

After having gone over some distance, Crimson Crest dropped down like one dead.

Meek Love wept, saying, "Ah, how he loved us!"

Bright Wit wept, saying, "Ah, how well he crowed!"

Fine Feather wept, saying, "Ah, what bright plumes he had!"

Crimson Crest some time after showed signs of life.

Meek Love cried, "Oh, live and love us again!"

Bright Wit cried, " Oh, let us hear your crowing again ! "

Fine Feather cried, " Oh, let us see your bright plumes again ! "

Then Crimson Crest got up like one waking from a trance, and with a hearty laugh exclaimed, " Ladies, you fancied you all loved me for one and the same reason ; but now you see, ' *There is many a way to love as they say !* ' "

THE FOX AND HIS SHADOW.

A FOX, one morning, found his shadow falling over a great part of the meadow. So said he to himself, " I must really be much bigger than I seem to be : certainly bigger than the elephant ! "

So, seeing an elephant pass by, he said, " You can't boast of your huge figure any more : behold, how big I am !—there is my shadow to prove it ! "

" If you were wise," said the elephant, " you would speak to my shadow."

The fox saw the shadow of the elephant stretching far beyond the meadow. He said, "Alas! *as one grows, so one's shadow.*"

THE SUN, THE WISE MEN, AND THE WAG.

Two men of great learning and wisdom, in the East, were one day discussing this point:—"Is it the same sun that rose yesterday that shines to-day, or some other orb every way similar to it?"

A wag, who heard this, addressed them as follows:—"Reverend sirs, I can easily solve the question, if you will permit me."

"By all means," said the wise men.

The wag then talked a great deal about the sun, and said, "To-morrow, the other half of my discourse will be delivered."

So the next day the wise men came to hear him, when the wag said, "Reverend sirs, I have my doubts as to your being the same wise men that spoke to me yesterday, and not some others every way similar to them. So, if you would satisfy me first on this point, I shall proceed with the other half of my lecture; else it would perhaps be thrown away!"

The wise men left the place to wrangle no more about the sun. The wag cried, "*Too much light dazzles the sight!*"

THE RAVEN AND THE CATTLE.

ONE evening, as some cattle were wending their way home, a raven rode on the horns of a bull in the herd; and as he approached the cottage, cried to the farmer, "Friend, my work for the day is over: you may now take charge of your cattle."

"What was your work?" said the farmer.

"Why," said the raven, "the arduous task of watching these cattle and bringing them home."

"Am I to understand you have been

THE RAVEN AND THE CATTLE,

[*Face p.* 56.

doing all the work for me?" said the farmer.

"Certainly," said the raven, and flew away with a laugh.

Quoth the farmer with surprise, "*How many there are that take credit for things which they have never done!*"

THE NYMPHS, LUCK AND ILL-LUCK.

Two nymphs, named Luck and Ill-luck, who lived in a wood, wished to know which of them was more beautiful than the other. They went to a fox in the wood, and asked him for his opinion.

He turned to them and said, "I can give no opinion unless you walk to and fro for a while."

So they did. Quoth the fox to Luck, "Madam, you are indeed charming when you come in." Quoth he to Ill-luck, "Madam, your gracefulness is simply inimitable when you go out!"

THE PEACOCK AND THE CROW.

A PEACOCK once stood before a mirror with his plumes spread, and said to it, "How grateful I am to you! But for you, I should not know how beautiful I am."

A crow, who heard this, said, "Sir Peacock, will the mirror tell me what I am like?"

"You are such an ugly thing, and yet you wish that a fine gentleman like the mirror should take the trouble of telling you how *you* look!"

But the crow went before the mirror, and found out what he was like. So he said, "*Be it a peacock or be it a crow, a mirror both doth truly show.* Yet how many there are that misrepresent the character of the good!"

THE MISER AND THE MONEY TREE.

IN the East, two men, whom we may call Rap and Tap, went to a miser's door, one evening, and began a conversation as follows :—

Rap. Brother, is this the house where the Sibyl said that the Money Tree grows?

Tap. Certainly, this is the house.

Rap. Perhaps by the Money Tree the Sibyl simply meant the wealth of the miser?

Tap. Oh, no; she distinctly said it is a tree with pence for leaves, shillings for flowers, and pounds for fruit, growing larger every hour, and is just ten feet below the great chest of the miser.

Rap. There is a genius guarding the tree, is there not?

Tap. Yes; and the only means of getting rid of him is to set the miser's chest at the gate, and shut the door, that the genius may turn to the chest, and let us have the tree. Else, the genius will certainly devour us, as the Sibyl said.

Rap. But what shall we do with the miser?

Tap. Why, squeeze his neck and bury him in the pit, after digging up the Money Tree.

Rap. But, as the tree may be rooted up, anyhow, this night, we shall go home and return better prepared.

So the two men pretended to leave the place and stood watching from a distance. The miser, who had heard the conversation, thought that if he should strive to get the Money Tree before them, he would be much more wealthy. He brought his chest out to beguile the genius, and went in to dig for the Money Tree.

Rap and Tap walked away with the chest, thinking they had better do so than wait for the Money Tree.

The miser, who had dug deep and not found the Money Tree, came out towards daydawn, and seeing his chest gone, wailed aloud. A great crowd gathered. Rap and Tap, who were among them, said, "*If money would grow, it must be so; if money would go, it must do so.*"

THE PIGS AND THE SAGE.

[Face p. 61.

THE PIGS AND THE SAGE.

ONCE a dozen pigs had to cross a stream. So the oldest of the herd said, "Now we are a dozen; when we go to the other bank, let us not forget to count and see that we are all right."

So they crossed over to the other side; and the leading pig counted his followers, and found they were eleven. "How is this? I counted twelve while on the other side!"

"One of us must have been drowned, or carried away by the stream," said the other pigs.

So there was great alarm in the herd for a while. A sage, who had been observing the scene from the opposite bank, laughed.

"May I know why you laugh, sir?" said the old pig.

"Because," said the sage, "you have furnished the only instance in which self was lost sight of—I mean, that self which is the first object of care all the world round!"

THE OWL AND THE ECHO.

An owl, puffed up with pride and vanity, was repeating his doleful cries at midnight from the hollow of an old oak. "How is it," he said, "that silence prevails in these woods, unless it be to allow my melodious voice to be heard with effect? Surely the groves are charmed with my voice! and when I sing, all nature listens."

An echo repeated the words, "All nature listens."

"The nightingale has usurped my rights," continued the owl; "his note is sweet—it is true; but mine is much more melodious."

"Much more melodious," repeated the echo.

Excited by approval, the owl, at the rising of the sun, instead of going to sleep as usual, continued to join his horrible hooting with the matin songs of other birds. But they were disgusted by the sounds, and with one consent attacked the owl and drove him from their society,

THE ASS AND THE WATCH-DOG.

[*Face p.* 63.

harassing him wherever he appeared, so that to escape from them he was glad to avoid the light and return to obscurity.

Vain people fancy that their imaginary perfections are the cause of admiration in others, and mistake their self-flattery for the voice of fame.

THE ASS AND THE WATCH-DOG.

A WATCH-DOG in a village was barking all night to keep thieves off from his master's house. An ass, who observed this, thought that the dog amused himself by barking. So he brayed all night. When the day dawned, the owner of the ass thought the poor animal had been suffering from some disorder. Therefore he sent for the village doctor, and laid the case before him.

The doctor examined the animal closely, and said, "Friend, you must brand this ass forthwith, else he will soon go into fits and die."

The ass said, "I assure you nothing is

wrong with me; I simply amused myself last night."

"Oh, no," said the inexorable leech; "I know what the wily brute means. He would rather die, and make you the loser, than be branded and recover his health."

So they bound the ass with ropes, and branded him all over with red-hot irons. Some time after the ass moved out to see how the village had fared during his illness. The dog asked why he had been branded. The ass narrated the story. Quoth the dog, "*He that mistakes work for amusement must pay for his error.*"

THE TIGER AND THE GIRAFFE.

A TIGER, named Old Guile, who had grown weak with age, was lying under a tree, by the side of a lake, in quest of some animal off which he could make a meal.

A giraffe, named Tall Stripes, who came to the lake to quench his thirst, attracted his attention, and Old Guile addressed him as follows:—"Oh, what a happy day! I see there the son of my old friend Yellow Haunch, who lived in the great forest near that distant mountain."

Tall Stripes was astonished to hear the words of Old Guile, and asked him how he, a tiger, was the friend of his father, a giraffe.

"I am not surprised at your question," replied Old Guile; "it is a truth known to very few indeed that the tiger and the giraffe belong to the same family. Just look at your skin and my own: yours is of a pale yellow colour—mine is very nearly the same; you have stripes—I have them, too. What more proofs do you want?"

Tall Stripes, who was extremely simple and guileless, believed these words, and said, "I am very happy to know that my father was your friend, and that we are of the same family. Can I do anything for you?"

Old Guile replied, "No, thank you; old

as I am, I make it a point of relying on myself. Further, a great part of my time is spent in prayer and meditation; for I consider it necessary, at this age, to devote all my attention to spiritual things. It will, however, be a great gratification to me to have your company whenever you should chance to pass by this lake."

Tall Stripes acceded to this request, and was about to go on his way, when Old Guile observed, "My dear Tall Stripes, you are well aware of the instability of all earthly things. I am old and infirm, and who knows what may happen to me to-morrow. Perhaps I may not see you again; so let me do myself the pleasure of embracing you before you leave me for the present."

"Certainly," said Tall Stripes. Thereupon Old Guile rose up slowly from his seat, like one devoid of all energy, and embracing him, plunged his deadly teeth into his long neck, and stretching him on the ground, made a hearty breakfast on him.

Beware of the crafty professions of the wicked.

THE TIGER, THE STAG, AND THE CROCODILE.

A STAG, named High Horn, went to a stream to quench his thirst. A tiger, named Long Leap, had been watching him from an adjacent bush. At the same time a monstrous crocodile, named Great Jaw, came to the edge of the water to seize the stag. High Horn had just finished drinking, when Long Leap darted at him, and Great Jaw drew near. But it so happened that Long Leap missed his prey and fell into the water, where Great Jaw caught him, and drew him down to the bottom of the stream. High Horn, who, a moment ago, had no idea of what the two animals had been planning, exclaimed, with a beating heart, "Ah, *the weak and the meek can never hope to live if the wicked do not destroy each other like these.*"

THE PEACOCK AND THE FOX.

A fox, who had an eye on a peacock, was one day standing in a field with his face turned up to the sky.

"Reynard," said the peacock, "what have you been doing?"

"Oh, I have been counting the stars," said the fox.

"How many are they?" said the peacock.

"About as many as the fools on earth," said the fox.

"But which do you think is the greater, the number of the stars or of the fools?" said the peacock.

"If you put it so, I should say the fools are more by one," said the fox.

"Who is that one?" said the peacock.

"Why, my own silly self!" said the fox.

"How are you silly, Reynard?" said the peacock.

"Why, was it not foolish of me to count the stars in the sky, when I could

THE PEACOCK AND THE FOX.

[*Face p.* 68.

have counted the stars in your brilliant plumage to better advantage!" said the fox.

"No, Reynard," said the peacock—"therein is not your folly—although there is neither wit nor wisdom in your prattle—but in the thought that your fine words would make an easy prey of me!"

The fox quietly left the place, saying, "*The knave that hath been found out cannot have legs too quick!*"

THE CAPTAIN, THE SOLDIER, AND THE HORSES.

A PARTY of soldiers, in the East, was in a wood one night, waiting for the enemy. The horses neighed. The captain said, "Kill them at once; else, the enemy is sure to know where we are, and run away."

An old soldier, to whom the order was given, took them behind the wood, and leaving them in charge of a comrade, returned saying, "Now we are safe."

Soon the enemy came near; but finding the party in the wood stronger, beat a hasty retreat. The captain, who was eager to pursue them, said, "What would I not give for the horses now!"

The soldier produced them at once. The enemy was pursued, and an important victory gained over them. The captain had the soldier raised from the ranks to a command in the army, observing, "Rashness is blindness. The future oft belies the present. *The prudent man hath eyes more than two.*"

THE DOG, THE WOLF, AND THE MOON.

ONE night a dog in charge of a flock of sheep was barking at the moon. A wolf who was lurking close by, said, "Why do you howl like that?"

"Because," said the dog, "I find you prowling here, and call to my friend in the moon to come down for a moment to help me to drive you away."

THE FOOL AND HIS FEVER.

[Face p. 71.

"Is there then a dog in the moon also?" said the wolf.

"Certainly there is one," said the dog.

"Any sheep?" said the greedy brute.

"None whatever," said the dog.

"Then it is not worth my while to go to the moon," said the wolf, and left the place.

The dog said, "*The greedy have ever an eye upon their prey!*"

THE FOOL AND HIS FEVER.

A FOOL was once suffering from severe fever. As he sat near the fire, he put the poker into it, and, after it was red hot, dipped it into a basin of water close by, and it was instantly cool. He rang for his servant, and ordering a tub full of cold water, went into it, and remained long enough to get rid of the heat in his body, as he thought.

When he came out, he was much worse. The doctor came and found him dying.

The fool told him how he thought he would cool down like the poker, and how he treated himself accordingly.

"Alas!" said the doctor, "*fools kill themselves by analogy!*"

THE ELEPHANT, THE FROGS, AND THE TOAD.

An elephant named Blackmound was in the habit of bathing in a great pond in a wood. The frequent visits of the elephant put the frogs in the pond to great inconvenience, and almost every day a number of them were crushed under his heavy feet.

Close by the pond in the hollow of a great tree lived the toad Blear Eye, who was remarkable for his wisdom. The frogs went up to him and said, "Blear Eye, not a day passes but some of us are killed by Blackmound. What shall we do?"

The toad replied, "Yes, I see your difficulty; the elephant is a bulky animal;

but you are little creatures, and you do not know that it is one thing to be bulky and another thing to be bold. However, I will try to help you. Allow me to select some one among you to execute my orders."

"Do help us, Blear Eye," cried the frogs with one voice.

Then Blear Eye called to his side a nimble frog named Lightfoot, and told him what he was to do.

Lightfoot went up to the top of a rock overhanging the pond and addressed Blackmound, who was just then coming towards it, from a distance, in the following terms: "You shall not come to the pond any more; for there is a spirit in yonder tree that has granted to me the power of shattering your huge frame."

"If so," said Blackmound, "I would like to hear the spirit say so, and to see you do it."

"Yes, we have granted the power to our faithful servant Lightfoot," said Blear

Eye, who was hidden within the hollow of the tree.

Before Blackmound could recover from his surprise at these words from an unknown quarter, Lightfoot leaped into the pond, where the shadow of Blackmound was reflected on the clear water, and cried, "Now I have done with your shadow: next your huge body shall disappear."

Blackmound was panic-struck, and thought that he would be destroyed, like his shadow, by the aid of the spirit in the tree, if he remained any longer at the place. So he beat a hasty retreat into the forest, never to return to the pond for any more baths; while the toad Blear Eye and the frogs shouted forth, "Hollo, Blackmound, *it is one thing to be bulky and another to be bold!*"

THE BLACK DOG AND THE WHITE DOG.

A MAN in the East once went about saying, "I can put these two dogs together, one of which is white, and the other black, as you see, and make a grey dog of them; and turn the grey dog again to the black dog and the white dog, if people would pay for the fun."

A wag who heard these words removed the two dogs at night, and left instead a grey cur. The man rose up in the morning and complained bitterly to the crowd, which came to see him, that some one had stolen his two dogs.

"No," said the wag, who was one of the crowd, "some one has simply saved you the trouble of putting the two dogs together, and making a grey dog of them. So you must now perform the other part of your trick, and make the black dog and the white dog out of this grey cur."

The man quietly threw his wallet over his shoulders and walked away. The wag and the crowd shouted—"The tongue hath no bone in it. It can turn as you twist it. *It is one thing to say, and another thing to do!*"

THE HARE AND THE PIG.

A HARE and a pig once agreed to leap over a ditch. The hare went a great way, and fell into it, just short by an inch. The pig went some way and fell into it; but far behind the hare. Yet they were eager to know which of them leapt more, and was therefore the better animal.

So they said to a fox, who had been watching the race, "Will you tell us which of us is superior, and which inferior, in the race?"

The fox said, "*Both in the ditch: can't say which!*"

THE ELEPHANT AND THE APE.

AN elephant named Grand Tusk and an ape named Nimble were friends.

Grand Tusk observed, "Behold, how big and powerful I am!"

Nimble cried in reply, "Behold, how agile and entertaining I am!"

Each was eager to know which was

THE ELEPHANT AND THE APE.

[Face p. 76.

really superior to the other, and which quality was the most esteemed by the wise.

So they went to Dark Sage, an owl that lived in an old tower, to have their claims discussed and settled.

Dark Sage said, "You must do as I bid, that I may form an opinion."

"Agreed!" cried both.

"Then," said Dark Sage, "cross yonder river, and bring me the mangoes on the great tree beyond."

Off went Grand Tusk and Nimble, but when they came to the stream, which was flowing full, Nimble held back; but Grand Tusk took him up on his back, and swam across in a very short time. Then they came to the mango-tree, but it was very lofty and thick. Grand Tusk could neither touch the fruit with his trunk, nor could he break the tree down to gather the fruit. Up sprang Nimble, and in a trice let drop a whole basketful of rich ripe mangoes. Grand Tusk gathered the fruit up into his capacious mouth, and the two friends crossed the stream as before.

"Now," said Dark Sage, "which of you is the better? Grand Tusk crossed the stream, and Nimble gathered the fruit. *Each thing in its place is best.*"

THE RAVEN, THE SERPENT, AND THE BRACELET.

A RAVEN had her nest on a tree; at the foot of the tree a serpent had its hole. The serpent went up the tree, and ate up the young birds in the raven's nest.

The raven said, "I am indeed very sorry that you have had to eat up my dear little ones for want of food. Should you be so good as to keep to your hole and leave my nest unmolested, I would give you every day a portion of the meal I get for myself."

The serpent, extremely irritated at this, replied, "You black, dirty thing that feeds on carrion, I would rather eat up your young ones and yourself than touch anything that you may fetch me."

The raven flew off to the palace, and taking up one of the bracelets of the queen, dropped it into the hole of the serpent. The servants of the royal household followed the bird, and dug into the hole to recover the bracelet. The serpent rushed out hissing at them, and was killed in a moment.

The wicked often fail to appreciate kindness in others, and compel them to work their ruin.

THE WASP AND THE PRINCE.

A WASP, named Pin Tail, was long in quest of some deed that would make him for ever famous. So one day he went into the king's palace, and stung the little prince, who was in bed. The prince awoke with loud cries. The king and his courtiers rushed in to see what had happened. The prince was yelling, and the wasp was stinging him again and again.

The king tried to catch him, and was stung; each of his courtiers tried in his turn to catch him, and was stung. Then the whole royal household rushed in, the news soon spread into the city, and the people flocked round the palace.

After much ado, the wasp was caught and flung on the ground, where he was severely hurt. He tried, however, to hold hard to a nook in the chamber, till the evening, when the servants that came to make the prince's bed said to one another, "The noise in the city has not yet ceased. They are still proclaiming with trumpet and drum the great event in the palace to-day."

"Yes," said one of the servants, "I hear their words clearly."

"What do they say?" said another.

"Why," said the former, "they say, a wasp named Pin Tail entered the palace, in spite of the guards, who watched at every gate, and stung the prince, the king, and his courtiers."

"The whole city," said his comrade, "is still in an uproar—all business suspended. Everybody is crying, 'Pin Tail, Pin Tail.' Never did such an event happen before!"

The wasp, which was about to die, heard these words, and expired exclaiming—"So, after all, Pin Tail hath done something which never happened before! That is gratifying! A name without fame is like fire without flame. *Nothing like attracting notice at any cost.*"

THE KING, THE QUEEN, AND THE PRIME MINISTER.

A KING, who was to choose a prime minister, had a person in view. The queen recommended a near relation, not qualified for the place. The king sent for both, and said, "What shall we do to one that spurns the king?"

The queen's man said, "There can be no greater crime than that: the person should have his feet cut off."

The king's man said, "A pair of shoes set with priceless gems should adorn the feet."

"How so?" said the impatient queen.

"May it please your majesty," said the statesman, "dare any touch the king with his feet other than the little prince that lies in your majesty's arms?"

The queen made no further objection to his appointment, saying, "Ah, *statesmen have to see, and to see through.*"

THE TIGER AND THE HARE.

A TIGER named Blind Fury became the king of a forest. He made a law that every day an animal should appease his hunger by falling a prey to him. At this rate, in the course of a few months, a great number of animals had been eaten up; the beasts that remained held a council.

THE TIGER AND THE HARE.

[Face p. 82.

A hare among them, named Tiny Trick, observed, "I have a stratagem whereby I can get rid of Blind Fury, if you would let me take my chance with him to-morrow."

They agreed. The usual breakfast hour of Blind Fury was nine; but Tiny Trick trudged on, and came to him at twelve.

"Hullo! you impudent little wretch! what keeps you so long from our presence?" said Blind Fury.

"May it please your majesty," said Tiny Trick, "in a well by the road I have travelled there is another king like your majesty. He said I should not go without appeasing his hunger. It was with difficulty I could obtain permission of him to see your majesty for a moment and return."

"Lead the way to the well," said Blind Fury.

"Yes, your majesty," said Tiny Trick.

When Blind Fury came to the well he found his own shadow reflected in it, and, fancying that it was another tiger, a rival, leapt into it and was drowned. The beasts of the forest praised Tiny Trick as the saviour of the state.

Little folk often do great things for the public good.

THE LUCKY MAN AND THE SEA.

Two men, one of whom was considered lucky, and the other unlucky, went out fishing in the sea. A storm arose, and upset their frail craft. They swam for their lives; but, as the shore was far, and the sea rough, they gave up all hope of seeing land again.

The man who believed himself specially unlucky said to the other, "But for me, you would be safe; it is my ill-luck that has raised the tempest."

While the other was endeavouring to reply, he felt a rock under the water, and stood upon it, as if in water knee-deep, and soon gave a helping hand to his companion. "Behold," said the latter, "*to the lucky man the sea is knee-deep!*"

THE LARK AND ITS YOUNG ONES.

A CHILD went up to a lark, and said, "Good lark, have you any young ones?"

"Yes, child, I have," said the lark; "and they are very pretty ones indeed!" Then she pointed to them, and said, "This is Fair Wing, that is Tiny Bill, and that other is Bright Eye."

The child said, "Yes, at home, we are three—myself and my two sisters, Jane and Alice; and mamma says we are pretty little children, and that she is very fond of us."

To this the little larks replied, "Oh yes, mamma is very fond of us too."

Then the child said, "Good lark, will you send home Tiny Bill to play with me?" Before the lark could reply, Bright Eye said, "Yes, if you will send little Alice to play with us in our nest."

The child said, "Oh, Alice will be so sorry to leave home, and come away from mamma!"

Bright Eye said, "Tiny Bill will be so sorry to leave our nest, and go away from mamma!"

The child was abashed, and went home, saying, "Ah, *every one is fond of home!*"

THE PEACOCK AND THE TORTOISE.

On a cloudy day, a peacock was dancing on a lawn by the side of a lake. A tortoise, in the lake, addressed the peacock thus—"Sir Peacock, how I should like to be with you dancing on the green turf!"

"Sir Tortoise," said the peacock, "I do not think you would be safe, if you were to leave the water, and to come to dance with me. Further, your short legs and heavy appearance would not enable you to cut a good figure at dancing."

"I see," said the tortoise, "you are very proud of your fine feathers and gait; but you must remember, that my shell is also as beautifully coloured; and that my gait, though not so quick and graceful, is yet slow and steady."

The peacock replied, "I am very sorry to have displeased you, Sir Tortoise; but, if you wish to come and dance with me, unmindful of the danger of leaving the water, you are welcome."

The tortoise came out of the lake, and stood by the side of the peacock, in his own awkward manner; and the two were preparing to dance together. Just then a hunter, who was passing by the pond, observing the scene, approached the animals. The peacock flew up a tree, and safely perched on its top; but the tortoise, before he could reach the pond, was laid on his back and killed by the hunter.

The peacock cried mournfully, "Sir Tortoise, you now see *how dangerous it is to get into difficulties from which we cannot easily escape.*"

THE CRANE, THE CRAB, AND THE FISH.

A CRANE that had long coveted the fish in a pond, one day stood on the bank in a melancholy mood.

"Sir Crane," said the fish in a shoal, "why are you sad to-day?"

"My dear fish," said Sir Crane, "I am so sorry that the fisherman is to come to-morrow with his net and take you all away."

"Oh, what shall we do?" cried the fish.

"Why," said the crane, "if you would only listen to my advice, you will all be saved."

"Do help us, by all means, Sir Crane; we will be so thankful to you," said the fish.

"Well, it may be a source of some trouble to me, but that is immaterial; when one can do a kind turn, he ought to do it. I shall take up as many of you as I can at a time, and carry you to a pond at some distance in a forest, where

THE CRANE, THE CRAB,
AND THE FISH.

[*Face p.* 88.

no fisherman can molest you." So saying, he carried each time a number of fish, and dropped them on a great piece of stone. There he made a hearty meal on as many as he could eat at a time, and left the remainder to dry in the sun.

It came to the turn of the crab to be carried. While the crane was flying in the air, the crab saw fish all the way, dried and drying. He cut asunder the neck of the crane with his sharp feet, and, falling into a pond, saved himself and the remaining fish in the pond he had left.

The wicked and the oppressor will find their doom in the end.

THE MAN AND THE VAULT.

A MAN in the East had continued reverses in trade, and owed a great many people large sums of money. So they took away all his property, leaving him in a very poor and miserable condition.

As he was hard pressed by hunger, he borrowed a spade of a neighbour, and dug up the stones in the pavement of his house that he might sell them and buy some food with the money. While turning up the stones in a room adjoining the garden, he found a vault underground, with a great chest in it.

He opened the chest, and found a vast amount of treasure, with a scroll. He poured forth his thanks to Heaven for the boon, and, opening the scroll, found these three sentences inscribed in letters of gold: (1) "Poverty leads to wealth." (2) "Misery leads to happiness." (3) "To them that trust in Heaven's power relief may come at the very last hour."

THE LOTUS, THE BEES, AND THE FROGS.

THE lotus in a pond blossomed. The bees swarmed to enjoy the sight and collect the honey. The frogs in the pond said, "You live so far from the pond: yet you come here so soon as the flowers blossom. How do you find it out ?"

"Why, by the sweet smell of the flowers," said the bees.

"We live in the pond, and yet we do not feel the smell. How is it ?" said the frogs.

"We can tell you of the smell, but we cannot furnish you with a nose to feel it," said the bees.

"Alas !" said the frogs, in a tone of self-reproach, "of what avail is it that frogs live by the lotus in the same pond if they cannot enjoy the sweet smell of the flower ? Yet there is nothing like acquiring the sense of what is fair and sweet."

So they requested the bees to teach them how to enjoy things fair and sweet.

"That is impossible, as we have already told you ; for a sense of 'fair and sweet,' you see, must be in us when we begin to be !" said the bees, and went about humming round the sweet lotus flowers.

THE CROW AND THE DAWN.

A CROW that lived on a tree by a great city in the East, thought that the day dawned because of his cawing. One day he said to himself, "How important I am! But for my care, I confess, the world would get into a mess."

He had a mind to see how the world would fare, if for it he did not care. So towards day-dawn, he shut his eyes, and slept away without cawing. Then he awoke, and found the sun shining as bright as ever on the great city.

He said, with great ill-humour, "I see how it happened. Some knave of my kind must have cawed and helped the sun up!"

Error breeds error.

THE TRADESMAN AND THE HONEST SERVANT.

A TRADESMAN in the East, who had not many customers, had a servant who was remarkable for speaking the truth. One day a gentleman came to the shop, and, finding everything in excellent order, said, "How well you arrange your things!"

"That is because we have not much business, sir—seldom any customers," said the servant.

The gentleman, who was struck by this remark, then asked for the quality of each of the various articles in the shop, and had a correct description from the honest servant. He bought a few things he wanted, and left the place.

The tradesman sent for the servant, and said, "You don't know how to get on in the world. You go and tell the gentleman we seldom have any customers. I can't hope to prosper with you. Leave me at once!"

The servant left the shop, and was engaged that very day by the owner of the opposite shop, who was in need of a servant. The next day the gentleman again called at the first shop, and said to the tradesman, "My friend, I have got a very large order to give, and to-morrow a great many of my friends intend buying here. Where is your honest servant? Unless he points out the articles I shan't be satisfied."

The tradesman was very sorry he had sent away the servant; but the gentleman soon found out he was in the opposite shop, and went there to make his purchases.

"Alas!" said the disconsolate tradesman, "what a lesson! *We ever profit by truth; but if ever we seem to lose, it is but the earnest of greater gain.*"

THE TIGER, THE FOX, AND THE HUNTERS.

A FOX was once caught in a trap. A hungry tiger saw him and said, "So you are here!"

"Only on your account," said the fox, in a whisper.

"How so?" said the tiger.

"Why, you were complaining you could not get men to eat, so I got into this net to-day, that you may have the men when they come to take me," said the fox, and gave a hint that if he would wait a while in a thicket close by he would point out the men to him.

"May I depend upon your word?" said the tiger.

"Certainly," said the fox.

The hunters came, and, seeing the fox in the net, said, "So you are here!"

"Only on your account," said the fox, in a whisper.

"How so?" said the men.

"Why, you were complaining you could not get at the tiger that has been devouring your cattle; I got into this net to-day that you may have him. As I expected, he came to eat me up, and is in yonder thicket," said the fox, and gave a hint that if they would take him out of the trap he would point out the tiger.

"May we depend upon your word?" said the men.

"Certainly," said the fox, while the men went with him in a circle to see that he did not escape.

Then the fox said to the tiger and the men, "Sir Tiger, here are the men; gentlemen, here is the tiger."

The men left the fox and turned to the tiger. The former beat a hasty retreat to the wood, saying, "I have kept my promise to both; now you may settle it between yourselves."

The tiger exclaimed, when it was too late, "Alas! *what art for a double part?*"

THE CLEVER MINISTER.

ONE day a king in the far East was seated in the hall of justice. A thief was brought before him; he inquired into his case, and said he should receive one hundred lashes with a cat-o'-ninetails.

Instantly he recollected an old Eastern saying,—

"What we do to others in this birth they will do to us in the next," and said to his minister, "I have a great mind to let this thief go quietly, for he is sure to give me these one hundred lashes in the next birth."

"Sire," replied the minister, "I know the saying you refer to is perfectly true, but you must understand you are simply returning to the thief in this birth what he gave you in the last."

The king was perfectly pleased with this reply, says the story, and gave his minister a rich present.

THE FARMER AND THE FOX.

A FARMER one morning noticed the footprints of some quadruped in his field, and said to a fox, "Reynard, my field was entered last night by some beast with four legs. Can you tell me which?"

"I am sorry I can't," said the fox, "but I know who can."

"Who is it?" said the farmer.

"There is a fish in the sea," said the fox, "that hath two fins; if you should ask him, he may tell you."

"What a silly reply!" said the farmer.

"Not more silly than the query," said the fox, as he retreated to the wood.

Consider twice before you put a question to a sly person.

THE KITES, THE CROWS, AND THE FOX.

THE kites and the crows made an agreement among themselves that they should go halves in everything obtained in the forest. One day they saw a fox that had been wounded by the hunters lying in a helpless condition under a tree, and gathered round it.

The crows said, "We will take the upper half of the fox."

"Then we will take the lower half," said the kites.

The fox laughed at it, and said, "I

always thought the kites were superior in creation to the crows; as such they must get the upper half of my body, of which my head, with the brain and other delicate things in it, forms a portion."

"Oh, yes, that is right," said the kites; "we will have that part of the fox."

"Not at all," said the crows; "we must have it, as already agreed." Then a war arose between the rival parties, and a great many fell on both sides, and the remaining few escaped with difficulty.

The fox continued there for some days, leisurely feeding on the dead kites and crows, and then left the place hale and hearty, observing, "*The weak benefit by the quarrels of the mighty.*"

THE FARMER AND THE FOX.

A FARMER was returning from a fair which he had attended the previous day at a neighbouring market town. He had a quantity of poultry which he had purchased. A fox observed this, and approaching the farmer said, "Good-morning, my friend."

"What cheer, old fellow?" said the farmer.

"I am just coming from the wood, through which you mean to go with your poultry. A band of highwaymen has been tarrying there since daybreak."

"Then what shall I do?" said the farmer.

"Why," said the fox, "if I were you I should stay here a while, and after breakfast enter the wood, for by that time the robbers will have left the place."

"So be it," said the farmer, and had a hearty breakfast, with Reynard for his guest.

They kept drinking for a long time. Reynard appeared to have lost his wits; he stood up and played the drunkard to perfection. The farmer, who highly admired the pranks of his guest, roared with laughter, and gradually fell into a deep slumber. It was some time after noon he awoke. But to his dismay he found that the fox was gone, and that the poultry had all disappeared!

"Alas!" said the farmer, as he trudged on his way home with a heavy heart, "I thought the old rogue was quite drowned in liquor like myself, but I now see it was all a pretence. *One must indeed be very sober to play the drunkard to perfection.*"

THE MAID AND THE WISE MAN.

A MAID in the East used to say, "Society is like a dish."

A wise man once heard these words, and said, "Fair maid, what do you mean?"

"Sir," said the maid, "if you wish to know what I mean, you must have dinner with me."

"Agreed," said the wise man.

The maid laid before the wise man plates of salt, pepper, fish, and other articles, each by itself. He could eat of none of these. Last of all, the maid brought a dish of curried fish, and the sage had his dinner.

"But where is the meaning of your saying?" said the sage.

"I have explained it," said the maid.

"I don't see it," said the sage.

"Why," said the maid, "you would not eat the salt, the pepper, the fish, each by itself; but when they came together, you had your dinner."

"You are quite right, fair maid," said the philosopher; "the salt is the witty man, the pepper the tart man, the fish the dull man, and, all together, make the one social man. *There is philosophy in the kitchen!*"

THE MAN AND HIS PIECE OF CLOTH.

A MAN in the East, where they do not require as much clothing as in colder climates, gave up all worldly concerns and retired to a wood, where he built a hut and lived in it.

His only clothing was a piece of cloth which he wore round his waist. But, as ill-luck would have it, rats were plentiful in the wood, so he had to keep a cat. The cat required milk to keep it, so a cow had to be kept. The cow required tending, so a cowboy was employed. The boy required a house to live in, so a house was built for him. To look after the house, a maid had to be engaged. To provide company for the maid, a few more houses had to be built, and people invited to live in them. In this manner a little township sprang up.

The man said, "*The farther we seek to go from the world and its cares, the more they multiply!*"

THE FOX AND THE DOVE.

A KING in the East had, on a lawn in his park, a great number of deer, all remarkable for their graceful appearance. A fox that had long had an eye on one of the fawns, said to the animals in the wood, "I have to go on a mission of importance to the king's park; but if I go in my own form, they will kill me. May I have the guise of any one of you that I may find it necessary to borrow?"

"Certainly," said the animals.

So the fox tried various forms, but failed in all. He sat brooding over his bad luck.

The wolf said, "Did not my form serve your purpose?"

"If I had gone in my own," said the fox, "I should have fared better."

Thus, after a great many animals had questioned him, and received some reply or other, the dove came up and said, "Surely with my guise it must have been otherwise?"

"Alas!" said the fox, "when I put on your guise, all thoughts of murder fled from my mind!"

The animals with one voice exclaimed, "*There is such virtue in goodness!*"

THE LION AND THE GOAT.

A LION was eating up one after another the animals of a certain country. One day an old goat said, "We must put a stop to

THE LION AND THE GOAT.

[Face p. 104.

this. I have a plan by which he may be sent away from this part of the country."

"Pray act up to it at once," said the other animals.

The old goat laid himself down in a cave on the roadside, with his flowing beard and long curved horns. The lion on his way to the village saw him, and stopped at the mouth of the cave.

"So you have come, after all," said the goat.

"What do you mean?" said the lion.

"Why, I have long been lying in this cave. I have eaten up one hundred elephants, a hundred tigers, a thousand wolves, and ninety-nine lions. One more lion has been wanting. I have waited long and patiently. Heaven has, after all, been kind to me," said the goat, and shook his horns and his beard, and made a start as if he were about to spring upon the lion.

The latter said to himself, "This animal looks like a goat, but it does not talk like one. So it is very likely some wicked spirit in this shape. Prudence often serves us better than valour, so for the present I shall return to the wood," and he turned back.

The goat rose up, and, advancing to the mouth of the cave, said, "Will you come back to-morrow?"

"Never again," said the lion.

"Do you think I shall be able to see you, at least, in the wood to-morrow?"

"Neither in the wood, nor in this neighbourhood any more," said the lion, and running to the forest, soon left it with his kindred.

The animals in the country, not hearing him roar any more, gathered round the goat, and said, "*The wisdom of one doth save a host.*"

THE SAGE AND THE ANIMALS.

THERE lived in the East a great sage who had the power of teaching any animal the tones of any other animal on earth. One day a great many animals went to him and received lessons.

Soon afterwards the fox presented himself before the poultry-yard, and crowed like Chanticleer. Chanticleer thought that some rival had come near ; so he went out to meet him. The fox got in by another way, and carried off as many of his hens and chicks as he could take.

The wolf went to the fold at night, and, bleating like a sheep, drew away from the flock a number of lambs, and made a hearty meal on them.

Then the kite, chirping merrily, tapped at the door of the sparrow's nest. The little sparrows cried, "Oh, mamma has just returned with something nice for breakfast!" and opened the door. The kite made his breakfast on them.

Thus every animal began to imitate the tones of some other, and do as much harm as possible. So they all went to the sage and told him of the result of their labours. "Ah," said the sage, "I thought as much.

You shall not have the power any more. *They that would abuse knowledge or power, should never get it.*"

THE TWO GEMS.

A DESPOT in the East once said to his fawning courtiers, "He that goes round my kingdom in the shortest possible time shall have one of these two gems."

A courtier went round the king, and said, "Sire, may I have the prize?"

"How so?" said the king.

"Why, you are the kingdom, are you not?" said the courtier.

The despot was so well pleased with the courtier that he gave him both the gems.

The other courtiers said, in a whisper, "*Flatterers prey upon fools.*"

THE CRANE AND THE FOOL.

IN the East there lived a fool, who went one day to his fields and said, "I sowed a month ago; should the crops stand two months more, I shall get three hundred bushels of corn. But I am in a hurry, so if I should reap now, I dare say I shall have one hundred bushels at least."

A crane who heard his words said, "If I were you, I should have all the three hundred bushels this very day."

"How?" said the fool.

"Why," said the crane, "you stored up water in the tank to feed the crops for three months. A month has elapsed, so water enough for two months more remains in the tank. Should you open the sluices and let all the water flow into the fields, you will have all the corn at once."

"Are you sure I shall have all the corn at once?" said the fool.

"Oh, yes," said the crane, "there is not the slightest doubt. My geographical knowledge is extensive, for I have travelled over a great part of the world; so you may depend on my world-wide knowledge and experience."

The fool then let all the water flow into

the fields. The crane invited his kindred, and they together ate all the big fish left in the tank first, and then, hovering over the fields, picked up all the small fish that had gone out with the water. A great portion of the crops was swept away; what remained was soon buried in the mud.

The fool sat on the bank of the lake and wept, saying, "The crane's geography ruined me."

"My friend," said the crane, "my geography was as good as your arithmetic. *It is all the same whether you fall into the ditch from this side or that!*"

THE SUN'S GRANDMAMMA.

THERE lived in the East a hag who used to say, "The sun sleeps every night in my house, and creeps back to the east to rise again." Should the morning be cloudy and the sun invisible, she would say, "My good man (meaning the sun) is yet sleeping; he is no doubt tired with the work he had yesterday."

A great many people believed her, called her the Sun's Grandmamma, and regarded her with great awe and respect. From time to time, when people wished to see the particular room in which the sun slept, she would take them in, for a fee, which she said the sun took to himself, and show them the door of a room under lock and key, which she called the sun's chamber.

Thus she made a large sum of money, which she kept in a great chest in the room. A wag, who had found out the secret, once went to her and said, "Madam, the sun bade me tell you he will be here this evening for dinner rather late."

Then he went about the neighbourhood and told the people that the sun was also to dine at the hag's house that evening. About midnight the people were startled to see the hag's house on fire, and herself wailing loud in these terms: "Alas! my chest has been stolen and my house burnt."

The wag, who had done this, and who

was one of the crowd, said, "All your fees went to the sun, so there could have been nothing in the chest. The sun said he would have his dinner here, so he has evidently been consuming the house."

The people said, "Just so!"

The hag said, "Gentlemen, I did not mean what I said; I had all the money. This wag has stolen my property."

The people said, "You did not mean what you said, and you do not say what you mean! 'Tis all the same," and dispersed.

Of course the hag let no more rooms to the sun!

THE LION, THE FOX, AND THE STORY-TELLER.

A LION who was the king of a great forest once said to his subjects, "I want some one among you to tell me stories one after another without ceasing. If you fail to find somebody who can so amuse me, you will all be put to death."

In the East there is a proverb which says, " The king kills when he wills." So the animals were in great alarm.

The fox said, " Fear not; I shall save you all. Tell the king the storyteller is ready to come to court when ordered." So the animals had orders to send the story-teller at once to the presence. The fox bowed respectfully, and stood before the king, who said, " So you are to tell us stories without ceasing ?"

" Yes, your majesty," said the fox.

" Then begin," said the lion.

" But before I do so," said the fox, " I would like to know what your majesty means by a story."

" Why," said the lion, " a narrative containing some interesting event or fact."

" Just so," said the fox, and began: " There was a fisherman who went to sea with a huge net, and spread it far and wide. A great many fish got into it. Just as the fisherman was about to draw the net the coils snapped. A great opening was made. First one fish escaped." Here the fox stopped.

"What then?" said the lion.

"Then two escaped," said the fox.

"What then?" said the impatient lion.

"Then three escaped," said the fox. Thus, as often as the lion repeated his query, the fox increased the number by one, and said as many escaped. The lion was vexed, and said, "Why, you are telling me nothing new!"

"I wish your majesty will not forget your royal word," said the fox. "Each event occurred by itself, and each lot that escaped was different from the rest."

"But wherein is the wonder?" said the lion.

"Why, your majesty, what can be more wonderful than for fish to escape in lots, each exceeding the other by one?"

"I am bound by my word," said the lion, "else I would see your carcass stretched on the ground."

The fox said in a whisper, "*If tyrants*

that desire things impossible are not at least bound by their own word, their subjects can find nothing to bind them."

THE DESPOT AND THE WAG.

A DESPOT in the East wished to have a great name as a very munificent prince, so he gave large presents to everyone of note that came to his court, but at the same time his officers had secret orders to waylay the recipients of his gifts and recover them.

In this manner many a man had been rewarded and plundered. Once a wag came to court, and amused him by his drolleries. The king gave him a great many presents, including a horse. After taking leave of the king and his courtiers, the wag bundled up the presents and put them over his shoulders, and mounting the horse, facing the tail, was going out. The king asked him why he acted in that manner.

"Sire," said the wag, "simply to see if your officers were coming behind, that I may at once hand over the bundle to them and go about my business."

The despot was abashed, and stopped giving any more presents, saying, "*Giving is but giving in vain, when we give to take again.*"

THE LION AND THE ELEPHANT.

A LION made great havoc on the animals under his control. They went up to a wise man in the forest and said, "Sire, the lion will soon empty the forest if he is not at once put down. We therefore beg of you to grant the elephant the power of putting down the lion."

"Yes," said the wise man.

The elephant became a very nimble and powerful beast of prey, and soon drove the lion out of the wood. Requiring, from his huge frame, a great deal more of nourishment than the lion, he began to kill a great many more animals in a day than the former. So the beasts again went up to the sage and said, "Sire, we pray you bid the elephant go back to his former condition, so that we may have the lion again for our king."

Said the sage, "Yes, *of two evils choose the less!*"

THE SUNLING.

IN the good old days a clown in the East, on a visit to a city kinsman, while at dinner, pointed to a burning candle and asked what it was. The city man said, in jest, it was a sunling, or one of the children of the sun.

The clown thought that it was something rare; so he waited for an opportunity, and hid it in a chest of drawers close by. Soon the chest caught fire, then the curtains by its side, then the room, then the whole house.

After the flames had been put down the city man and the clown went into the burnt building to see what remained.

The clown turned over the embers of the chest of drawers. The city man asked what he was seeking for. The clown said, "It is in this chest that I hid the bright sunling; I wish to know if he has survived the flames."

"Alas," said the city man, who now found out the cause of all the mischief, "*never jest with fools!*"

THE GENTLEMAN AND THE SEDAN BEARERS.

In the good old days a gentleman in the East one day missed his dog. He sent for his sedan bearers, and asked them to go in quest of it.

They said, "We are not here to seek for your dog, but simply to bear your sedan."

"You are perfectly right," said the gentleman, "so I shall go in quest of the dog; bring up the sedan at once." The gentleman got into his sedan, and the men had to take him over hill and dale till they were quite tired. They then said with one voice, " Sir, we beg of you to stop; we can hardly stand on our legs any more. If you wish to seek for the dog farther, we shall go in quest of it."

" Do so," said the gentleman, smiling, and walked home.

" Alas," said the men as they sat down under a tree to rest their weary limbs, "*often mending is but marring.*"

THE LION AND THE GADFLY.

ONCE a lion was sleeping in his den at the foot of a great mountain. A gadfly that had been sipping the blood and froth from his mouth bit him severely. The lion started up with a roar, and catching the fly in his huge paws, said, " Villain, you are at my mercy! How shall I punish your impudence?"

" Sire," said the fly, " if you would pardon me now, and let me live, I shall be able to show ere long how grateful I am to you."

"Indeed," said the lion; "who ever heard of a gadfly helping a lion? But still I admire your presence of mind and grant your life."

Some time after, the lion, having made great havoc on the cattle of a neighbouring village, was snoring away in his den after a heavy meal. The village hunters approached with the object of surrounding him and putting an end to his depredations.

The fly saw them, and hurrying into the den, bit the lion. He started up with a roar as before, and cried, "Villain, you will get no pardon this time!"

"Sire," said the fly, "the village hunters are on their way to your den; you can't tarry a moment here without being surrounded and killed."

"Saviour of my life!" said the lion as he ran up the mountain. "*Nothing like forgiving, for it gives the humblest an opportunity of helping the highest.*"

THE SAGE AND THE CHILDREN.

A SAGE in the East once went to a certain country, where he saw this : The children said they were hungry; the mothers cooked their breakfast and placed it before them.

Just as the children were putting the food to their lips a number of rude men rushed in and carried off the dishes. The mothers quietly observed the scene without complaining, nor did the children make any stir.

The sage was surprised, and asked what all that meant. The mothers said, "Sir, we beseech you to observe a while more." Then the children started, and went about seeking for their breakfast, which the men had hidden somewhere, and after much ado got it and appeased their hunger.

The mothers turned to the sage, and said, "Sir, in our country it is thus we teach our children early the great virtue of patience. *That which really leads men to success is the faculty of putting up with disappointment in the early part of their career.* It is thus we cultivate the faculty in our children."

THE MUSHROOM AND THE GOOSE.

A GOOSE that was once cackling with great pride thought that a mushroom was gazing at it, and said, "You contemptible thing, why do you stare at me like that? You can never hope to meet me on terms of equality, can you?"

"Certainly, madam," said the mushroom, "and that very soon."

This enraged the goose more, so she said, "I would cut you up to pieces with my bill but for the people who are close by, and who are so silly as to care for you," and went strutting away. Soon after the goose and mushroom were served up in separate dishes, very near each other.

"Ah," said the mushroom, "you see we have met after all, and so closely. *Those who have a common fate in the end had better be friends.*"

THE FOX IN A WAREHOUSE.

A FOX once entered a merchant's warehouse, and finding nothing to his taste, was quietly going out. The merchant, who wished to have a joke with him, said, "My dear sir, may I know what you wish to purchase?"

"I am afraid you have it not," said the fox.

"What! we have everything, from a needle to an anchor," said the merchant. "That is just what I want," said the fox. "If you have a needle as big as an anchor, and an anchor as small as a needle, you will oblige me!"

"Ah!" said the merchant; "*in war and wit, they win by a hit!*"

THE COBBLER AND THE TURKEY.

A COBBLER once paid a visit to a farmer. The turkey in the farmyard began to cackle. The cobbler snatched a stick and ran towards the fowl.

"What are you going to the turkey for?" said the farmer.

"Why," said the man, "the silly fowl hath no manners. I stand here and it says 'Gobble, gobble, gobble.'* I mean to teach it a lesson!"

"Ah!" said the farmer; "how many there are that would not be called by their right names!"

THE FROG AND THE KING.

A GREAT drought prevailed in a country in the East at one time. There was hardly any water to drink. In the chief city there was a great cistern, from which water was measured out every day to the people in the town and in the provinces.

One night the watchman came running to the king and said, "Sire, there has been a leak somewhere in the cistern, and the water is flowing out."

* The word in the East is "chuckle."

The king, with all his court, came out to see the leak, but it could not be discovered. However, some time after, the water ceased to flow. Still, to make sure that all was right, the next day the spot where the leak had happened was carefully examined. The workmen found out the hole, and saw a frog blocking it up.

They were about to fling the frog on the ground with violence, when the king said, "Oh, no, he is our benefactor; but for him all the water would have gone out." The workmen laid him gently on the ground, and he escaped into the cistern, saying to the king, "Sire, *to discover merit in the lowly is harder work than ruling over a kingdom.*"

THE FISH AND RAIN.

THE water in a lake was fast drying up. The fish were all alarmed. A meeting of the animals in the lake was held. The crocodile, as the most powerful among them, took the chair. The tortoise made a long speech, and concluded by saying, "Therefore it is, I do not care whether it is land or water. It is the same to me; I can live in either."

The crab made another long speech, and, in the end, observed, "No less with me, brethren. Should the lake dry up I will go to the neighbouring fields and live in the holes." The snails, the leeches, the water-snakes, and various other animals, gave some excuse or other to keep away from praying for rain.

The crocodile summed up, saying, "I care not where I live. On land I find better food than in water, for you must all admit that a hare, or rabbit, or some other land animal of the kind, is much better fare than fish or frogs." At this there was loud applause, and the meeting came to an end.

But the poor fish, who could not live out of water for one moment, thought it their duty, however, to pray; so they did.

Very soon the sky was overcast, the clouds poured, and the lake was full. All the animals rejoiced at it. The fish, with heartfelt pride and pleasure, observed, "*Heaven blesseth the many for the few!*"

THE VIPER IN THE KING'S GARDEN.

A KING in the East had a beautiful garden close to his palace, of which he took great care. One day a viper got into it. A servant of the palace, who saw it entering, reported the matter to the king.

His majesty expressed great concern at it, and sending for his chief gardener, said, "You see the garden is close to the palace. We occupy this suite of chambers, the ladies of our household the next, the little princes and princesses the third; so the viper should be caught and destroyed at any cost before nightfall, otherwise not one of us will have a wink of sleep to-night. Mind! we would even have all the trees and the bushes in the garden rooted up, if need be, to see if the animal has got into any of the holes or cavities under them, although we have fostered them so long for our pleasure with paternal care, for you know the proverb which says, 'Life first, pleasure next.'"

The gardener obeyed. He and his men sought for the viper all round, but nowhere could it be found; so they rooted up, one after another, the trees and plants in the garden till not a blade of grass was left standing. A huge pile was formed of all the vegetation thus destroyed. At last, within a hole, under the foot of a lovely hawthorn which had just been cut down, was the malicious reptile snugly coiled up. Instantly the gardeners killed it and brought it to the king.

His majesty viewed the dead snake with satisfaction, but turning to the green pile in the garden, with a heavy heart exclaimed, "*Alas, the wickedness of one hath ruined a host!*"

THE HAMMER AND THE ANVIL.

ONCE the hammer said to the anvil, "I can strike harder than you can bear."

The anvil replied, "I can bear harder than you can strike; try!"

The hammer redoubled its energy, and the anvil was as firm as ever.

"Hold on, gentlemen!" said the iron that had got between the two, "the world gains by it."

"Quite right," said the furnace, in its own abrupt style; "vie and win; *competition is the secret of the world's success.*"

W. Jolly & Sons, Printers, Bridge Street, Aberdeen.